WORKFORCE: BUILDING SUCCESS

PROBLEM SOLVING

Project Consultant

Harriet Diamond
Diamond Associates
Westfield, NJ

Series Reviewers

Nancy Arnold
Metropolitan Adult
Education Program
San Jose, CA

Lou Winn Burns
Booker High School
Sarasota, FL

Jane Westbrook
Weatherford ISD
Community Services
Weatherford, TX

Ronald D. Froman
National Training &
Development Specialists
Winter Springs, FL

Dr. Randy Whitfield
North Carolina Community
College System
Raleigh, NC

Ann Jackson
Orange County
Public Schools
Orlando, FL

STECK-VAUGHN
ELEMENTARY · SECONDARY · ADULT · LIBRARY

A Harcourt Company

www.steck-vaughn.com

Acknowledgments

Steck-Vaughn Company
Executive Editor: Ellen Northcutt
Supervising Editor: Tim Collins
Senior Editor: Julie Higgins
Assistant Art Director: Richard Balsam
Design Manager: Danielle Szabo

Proof Positive/Farrowlyne Associates, Inc.
Program Editorial, Development, Design, and Production

Photo Credits
Cover Photo: © FPG
Pp. 14, 30, 37, 45, 53, 55, 61, 62, 70, 79 © From: The ENTER HERE® Series, © 1995 by Enter Here L.L.C.; p. 4 © Marie Mills/David Cummings/Unicorn Stock; p. 7 © 1996 Park Street; p. 12 © Charles Gupton/Tony Stone Images; p. 13 © Bob Sollars/Unicorn Stock Photos; p. 20 © Dick Young/ Unicorn Stock Photos; p. 21 © 1996 Park Street; p. 23 © 1996 Park Street; p. 28 © Chromosohm/Sohm/Unicorn Stock Photos; p. 29 © Mark Richards/PhotoEdit; p. 36 © Barbara Filet/Tony Stone Images; p. 39 © 1996 Park Street; p. 44 © Myrleen Ferguson/ PhotoEdit; p. 46 © Jon Riley/Tony Stone Images; p. 52 © Amy C. Etra/PhotoEdit; p. 60 © Tony Freeman/PhotoEdit; p. 68 © Michael Newman/PhotoEdit; p. 76 © Michael Newman/ PhotoEdit; p. 78 © 1996 Park Street.

ISBN 0–8172–6520–1

Contents

To the Learner

Workforce: Building Success is a series designed to help you improve key job skills. You will find many ways to improve your skills, whether you're already working or are preparing to find a job. This book, *Problem Solving,* is about using your skills to identify and solve problems. You will need to solve problems in your own work and with your work team.

Before you begin the lessons, take the Check What You Know skills inventory, check your answers, and fill out the Preview Chart. There you will see which skills you already know and which you need to practice.

After you finish the last practice page, take the Check What You've Learned inventory, check your answers, and fill out the Review Chart. You'll see what great progress you've made.

Each lesson is followed by four types of exercises:

- The questions in **Comprehension Check** will help you make sure you understood the reading.
- In **Making Connections,** you will read about situations in which people need to use the skills in the reading.
- In the next section, called **Try It Out, Act It Out,** or **Talk It Out,** you will complete an activity that requires you to use the new skills. You might interview someone, conduct a survey, make a telephone call, have a discussion, or role-play a situation.
- In **Think and Apply,** you will think about how well you use the skills in your daily life. Then you will decide which skills you want to improve and make a plan to reach your goal.

At the end of the book, you will find a Glossary and an Answer Key. Use the Glossary to look up definitions of key work-related words. Use the Answer Key to check your answers to many of the exercises.

Check What You Know will help you know how well you understand problem-solving skills. It will also show you which skills you need to improve.

Read each question. Circle the letter before the answer.

1. Penny works in a photocopy shop. She has three main responsibilities. She helps walk-in customers, she answers the phone, and she works on large copying projects that customers drop off. When the shop is busy, she cannot do all three tasks. What is important for her to do to solve this problem?

   a. She should always help walk-in customers first.

   b. She should figure out which jobs need to be worked on right away and which can be worked on later.

   c. She should ask the management to buy another copying machine.

2. Cassius is a supervisor in an auto body repair shop. He wants to figure out how to offer lower repair bills. He starts by writing down all the labor and materials costs in customers' bills. His next step should be to

   a. reduce prices on materials.

   b. find out which kinds of costs might be reduced.

   c. predict the results.

3. If you have a plan for finishing your work by the end of the day, and your plan doesn't work, you should

   a. not complete that work because you don't have time.

   b. move on to something else.

   c. make a second backup plan.

4. Gordon, Mary, and Isabel use computers to perform their work. Who has the best attitude about using computers?

   a. Gordon says that if a computer can't solve a problem, then there is no solution.

   b. Mary tries to learn as much as she can about the new software at her job.

   c. Isabel figures that the less she has to do with computers, the better.

5. Alicia works behind the counter in a gift shop. It is the holiday season and she is feeling stressed by her workload. What would be important for her to do during this period?

a. Get enough sleep.

b. Slow down at work.

c. Take on more overtime.

6. Sarah needs to solve a problem with a coworker, Noah. Noah does not recycle his paperwork. If Sarah talks to him, Noah might start recycling. If she talks to him, he might be offended. If she doesn't, he will continue not to recycle. The best thing for Sarah to do is

a. forget about it and see if Noah starts to recycle on his own.

b. tell Noah that he must start to recycle or he'll lose his job.

c. solve the problem by talking to Noah.

7. Jason is part of a road crew that is repairing city streets. The crew's plan is to complete the work on ten different blocks during the summer. This summer there have been many heavy rainstorms that have slowed the work. At this point, Jason's crew has to come up with a new plan. This passage is an example of

a. a lazy crew.

b. the difficulties of outdoor work.

c. a work team being able to work with changes.

8. Nina works in a large textile plant. The people who work there are of many different nationalities. To get along with her coworkers, it is especially important for Nina to

a. respect the ways that other people do things.

b. ignore the differences.

c. try to act like whomever she is working with at the time.

9. Steven stopped at the corner store to buy some items for the office. The store shelf does not have the items he needs. Steven should

   a. leave and come back another time.
   b. write a note requesting the item and leave the note on the counter.
   c. ask the store manager or clerk if the item is in stock.

10. Terry manages the Big Slice pizza shop. The shop has not been getting much business lately. Most people are going to another pizza shop across the street. Several of the employees at Big Slice are familiar with the neighborhood and might have some ideas that could help revive Big Slice's business. What should Terry do next?

    a. Get all the employees together to exchange ideas.
    b. Hire new employees.
    c. Hire a designer to redecorate the front of the shop.

Preview Chart

This chart will show you what skills you need to study. Reread each question you missed. Then look at the appropriate lesson of the book for help in understanding the correct answer.

Question Check the questions you missed.	Skill The exercise, like the book, focuses on the skills below.	Lesson Preview what you will learn in this book.
1._____	Listing high-priority and low-priority tasks	4
2._____	Creating a list of possible solutions	2
3._____	Creating backup plans	5
4._____	Viewing technology changes in a positive way	8
5._____	Taking care of yourself	10
6._____	Weighing the advantages and disadvantages	3
7._____	Being flexible in responding to challenges	7
8._____	Understanding cultural differences	9
9._____	Gathering information	1
10._____	Brainstorming to create ideas	6

Identifying Problems

What kinds of problems do people have at work?

How do you identify problems?

Identifying problems carefully is the first step in solving them.

Problems are a part of life. Problems can be understood as opportunities or challenges. In the workplace, your success is measured, in part, by your ability to solve problems. There is a process of steps that you can follow to meet a problem and solve it. This lesson presents the first step in the process, which is identifying the problem.

Identify Problems

To **identify** means to recognize. To identify a problem, you need to realize that it exists. You need to

4

understand it. A **problem** is a confusing or difficult situation or question. Problems at work may be about reaching goals, satisfying customers, and making a good product. For example, suppose a coworker is often late for your regular Monday meetings. Without the meeting, you cannot perform your work for the day. You have a problem with that coworker. You need to talk with him or her to make clear the importance of meeting on time. The following tips can help you identify problems in the workplace and understand them.

Gather information. In the workplace, problems can be caused by people, processes, or pieces of equipment that aren't working well. Learn about the people. Learn about the equipment and the process. For example, suppose you work in a department store. Your register is not reading the price label on a product. You need to trace the source of this problem. Has the stockperson put on the wrong labels? This problem may be traced to a process. Perhaps a coworker gave the stockperson the wrong label information. Or perhaps the problem is the equipment. Gather information about the different parts of the problem.

Organize information. Put the information into **categories,** or groups. Items in a category have something in common. You might have categories for problems caused by workers, processes, and equipment.

Interpret the information. What does the information mean? Why did the problem happen? Is the problem large or small? Does it affect many people or just a few? Once you have interpreted what the information means, you will be able to start working on a solution. The following case study shows how Priscilla begins gathering information to understand a problem.

Priscilla works on a production line at REbound Athletic Shoes Company. She is meeting with Tomás Herrera, the plant supervisor.

Tomás: I know all of you work hard. But we need to find a way to increase production. We are not meeting our goals.

Priscilla: How much are we off our goals?

Tomás: Each day this plant produces about 10,000 pairs of shoes. That's 500 fewer pairs than other REbound plants produce in a day. We have a production problem. We need to find the cause of the shortage. Priscilla, I'd like you to be in charge of your team on this. Would you begin observing the production area and gathering information? Try to find out why production is low.

Tomás has identified the problem. But he does not understand the causes or reasons for it. Priscilla asks a question to gather more information about the problem. Next, she needs to gather information from workers, organize the information, and interpret it. Then, she can begin to look for causes and solve the problem.

Use Problem-Solving Steps

Once you identify and understand a problem, you need to take steps to solve it. Lessons 2–5 show the other steps in the problem-solving process. Lesson 2 explains analyzing the problem and finding causes. Lesson 3 presents ways to create solutions to the problem. In Lesson 4, you will learn how to put your solution into action with a plan. Lesson 5 shows you how to review and revise your plans. Sometimes you might have to try many solutions before you find the one that works, as shown in the following case study.

Case Study

Kerri is a special events coordinator for a hotel. She is helping a couple, Pam and Chet, plan their wedding reception. Planning this reception is Kerri's work problem to solve. The bride and groom have many requirements for their reception. They want to keep their costs low. They want to have dancing and food. They changed the number of guests from 50 to 75 people. This increase changed the costs for the reception. Kerri talks to Pam on the telephone.

Communicating changes in plans helps avoid problems.

Pam: We liked the Emerald Room the best. We'd like to reserve that room for the reception.

Kerri: That's a very nice room, but it's a bit small for 75 people.

Pam: It seemed like it would be big enough. Anyway we can't afford any other room.

Kerri: Maybe we need to think more about the room and the number of people you've invited.

Kerri is worried that there won't be enough space for everything the couple and their guests want to do. If they have a sit-down dinner, there will be just enough room for all the tables. But Pam and Chet want to have dancing, too. There won't be any room for that. Now Kerri must work on finding a new solution. She needs to find a solution before she can put it into action.

You will face problems in the workplace. The way you deal with those problems can make all the difference. Being able to identify problems is the first step toward solving them. Read about the other steps in the problem-solving process in Lessons 2–5. The later lessons introduce other challenges in the workplace that you can meet with problem-solving steps.

Comprehension Check

Complete the following exercises. Refer to the lesson if necessary.

A. What is a problem?

_____

B. List three ways to help identify a problem.

1. _____

2. _____

3. _____

C. List five problem-solving steps.

1. _____

2. _____

3. _____

4. _____

5. _____

D. Complete each sentence. Circle the letter in front of the answer.

1. The first step in problem solving is

   a. identifying the problem.

   b. getting a memo from your boss.

   c. putting a plan into action.

2. Problems are also

   a. opportunities.

   b. solutions.

   c. information.

Answer the questions following each case. Then talk about your answers with your partner or group.

Case A

Joel Harrison owns Harrison's Fresh Pretzels. Lately, he has noticed that his production area is producing fewer pretzels. The bakery produces 100 pretzel packages a day. It should produce 150 packages to meet customers' needs. Many customers tell him that the quality of the pretzels seems better. Joel speaks with Jeritha, the head baker, to learn about the production. Jeritha reminds Joel that he decided to add butter to the recipe. The butter makes the pretzels taste better. However, the process for adding the butter slows down the production process.

1. Does Joel have a problem? If so, what is it?

   _____

   _____

   _____

   _____

2. What does Joel do to learn about production?

   _____

   _____

   _____

Case B

Sarena works at an auto factory. She is the leader of her work group. She and three other workers install the steering wheel and dashboard in new cars. Lately, Sarena has noticed that her work group doesn't get along well. There is a lot of arguing. Sometimes the workers are rude to each other. Sarena ignored the problem at first. But now it has become too unpleasant.

What should Sarena do about this problem?

_____

_____

Case C

Aidan supervises several office clerks at the state courthouse. The clerks keep track of the records for all court cases. Lately, some of the files have been put in the wrong place. Others are missing. Several people have complained, but Aidan has ignored them. He knows there is a problem but feels that there is no way to avoid it. He says his office is too busy to keep up with the filing. He decides to ignore the problem.

1. Has Aidan identified a problem?

_____

2. What should Aidan's next step be?

_____

TRY IT OUT

Visit a business in your community. Interview a manager at the company. Ask questions about how the manager identifies problems. How does he or she use information to help solve those problems? Does he or she have any special problem-solving strategies? Share your information with the rest of your class.

Think and Apply

How well do you use the skills in this lesson? Complete these exercises.

A. Think about what you learned in this lesson and answer the questions. Share your answers with your partner or your class.

1. Describe three problems you have had at home, at school, or in the workplace.

   a. _____

   b. _____

   c. _____

2. How did you identify each problem from question 1?

   a. _____

   b. _____

   c. _____

3. Ask a friend to tell you what you might have done differently to solve each problem. What was your friend's advice?

   _____

B. Review your answers to A. Complete the checklist. Then answer the questions that follow.

1. Read the list of skills. Check the boxes next to your strengths.

   ☐ identifying problems

   ☐ gathering information

   ☐ organizing information

   ☐ interpreting the information

   ☐ using problem-solving strategies

2. Do you want to improve any of your skills? Which ones?

   _____

3. How do you plan to improve the skills you listed in question 2?

   _____

Finding Causes of Problems

Once a problem is identified, the next step is to find out its cause.

There is a lot more to solving a problem than just identifying it. The next step is to analyze the problem. To **analyze** means to examine closely or break into parts. In examining a problem, you might look for the cause. This lesson presents methods to analyze problems.

Consider Causes of the Problem

Try to think of *every* possible cause for the problem. As you think of causes, write them down. Try to list at least five causes. For example, suppose you have a problem with a cash register at work. The register tape often does not print the purchases on the receipt tape. You list five possible causes for the problem as follows:

1. The tape ribbon should be replaced.
2. The printer inside the register is not working.
3. The tape is not moving to the printer in the register.
4. The tape and ribbon are poor quality.
5. Coworkers are not using the register properly.

Then review your list of causes. Delete any causes that don't seem possible or that you can "rule out." For example, if you have used the same kind of tape and ribbon for a year and the register has worked, you could cross off the fourth cause from your list. Then investigate the causes left on your list. Use them as a guide to analyze the problem. Read the following case study to see how Priscilla tries to list possible causes for her production problem.

You may use problem-solving skills to help you get a machine running properly.

Case Study

At the REbound Athletic Shoes plant, Priscilla is trying to find out why productivity is low. She is working with her team in the production department. She is trying to find out why the department is not producing enough shoes. She must analyze the problem and find causes. Priscilla meets with her production team. Together they create a list of possible causes of the problem. They try to think of every possible cause. Here is their list:

1. Not enough workers

2. Workers working too slowly

3. Materials not available

4. Equipment breaks down

5. Not enough equipment

Priscilla reviews the completed list. She needs to delete causes that are not possible.

Research the Causes

In Lesson 1, you learned that you can gather information to help you identify a problem. You can also gather information to learn about causes. You need to look for clues that prove one or more of your causes is correct. There are several ways to do this. One way is by **observing,** which means to look closely at *what* is done

To learn about causes, gather information from coworkers and outside sources.

and *how* it's done. Suppose the people you work with are not using the cash register properly. One clerk tears off the tape too quickly. Does this cause the register not to print?

Another way to gather information is to gather it from coworkers. Ask questions. What do they think about the problem? What do they think is the cause? Ask for opinions and facts.

You might also check some outside sources. Contact other departments within your company. Maybe those departments have experienced the same problem. If you are having a problem with equipment, you could contact the company that sells or makes that equipment. Gather information so you can fix your problem.

The following case study shows how Priscilla gathers information from outside sources and coworkers.

Case Study

Priscilla calls two other REbound plants. She learns that the other plants use the same number of machines. She also learns that the other plants employ the same number of people on the production line. She realizes that "not enough equipment" and "not enough workers" are not causes. She deletes the first and fifth causes. She focuses on the three remaining items on the list.

Priscilla watches her team of employees at work. They do not waste time. They communicate and help each other complete their tasks. Priscilla deletes the second cause, "workers not working well," from her list. All members of the production team tell Priscilla that they do not have the necessary materials for their work. One coworker tells her that the equipment breaks down for twenty minutes at least twice a day. In other words, the equipment is down for at least forty minutes a day.

Priscilla writes this down. She meets with Tomás to give him the information. She tells him that there are two causes. First, the necessary materials are not available to workers. Second, the equipment breaks down. She and Tomás decide that they can begin solving the production problem based on the two causes she has found.

It is not enough to find causes to problems. You need to research the causes to stay on the right track. If you have information pointing to specific causes, you can begin to prepare a solution, which is the subject of Lesson 3. Use research to guide the way you analyze problems and find causes.

Comprehension Check

Complete the following exercises. Refer to the lesson if necessary.

A. What does analyze mean?

_____

B. How can you consider possible causes of a problem?

_____

_____

C. List three things you can do to research causes.

1. _____

2. _____

3. _____

D. Mark the following statements T (True) or F (False).

_____ 1. Outside sources of information may help you find causes of a problem.

_____ 2. Coworkers cannot help you find causes of a problem.

E. Complete each sentence. Circle the letter in front of the answer.

1. The first step in analyzing a problem is

   a. observing.
   b. creating a list of possible causes.
   c. eliminating unreasonable causes.

2. To analyze means to

   a. examine closely and break into parts.
   b. create a solution.
   c. review your options.

Making Connections

Answer the questions following each case. Then talk about your answers with your partner or group.

Case A

Ellis supervises a team of patrol officers. He has noticed that one of his trainees, Lola, is very slow in an emergency. She takes a long time to get ready to go out on the job. She has also made a lot of mistakes on the job. Ellis thinks Lola hasn't been listening well to his instructions. Ellis is worried about Lola. He can't keep a patrol officer who doesn't understand the job.

How should Ellis research the causes for Lola's poor performance?

_____

_____

_____

Case B

Drexel has worked for two years as an EKG technician. The doctors have a very high opinion of Drexel. For the past three days, Drexel has been having trouble with the department computer. A few times he has been unable to find information about a patient. Drexel likes his job and he wants to do well. He knows that accurate information is very important. He doesn't know if the problem is with him or with the computer. So far he hasn't talked to anyone about the problem. One of the doctors he works with has noticed that something is wrong. This doctor asks Drexel what the problem is. Drexel has to tell her he doesn't know.

1. What advice would you give Drexel? How can he find the cause of his problem?

_____

_____

2. List at least three possible causes of Drexel's problem.

_____

_____

_____

Case C

Claire works for a catalog company. She has been with the company for three years. She fills orders by packing and shipping boxes of merchandise. She is very good at her job. Recently the company expanded. Claire works at a new warehouse. It is much larger than the old one. It has many more kinds of merchandise. Claire has a new manager. During the first month in the new warehouse, Claire's productivity goes down.

List at least three possible causes.

_____

_____

_____

TALK IT OUT

Work in small groups. Each person will describe a problem to the group. The problem can be real or made up. It can be a personal problem or a problem about school or work. As a group, create a list of possible causes for the problem. Then discuss the list as a group. Do any causes seem unreasonable? Cross those off the list. Then discuss possible ways to find out more about the problem's causes.

Think and Apply

How well do you use the skills in this lesson? Complete these exercises.

A. Think about what you learned in this lesson and answer the questions. Share your answers with your partner or your class.

1. Think of a problem you have had as a customer of a business. Some examples might be a store that doesn't have a return policy or a repair person who doesn't show up on time. What were some of the possible causes of the problem?

   _____

   _____

   _____

2. Talk to a partner about a problem you had to figure out in the past. Be sure to choose a problem in which the cause wasn't clear at first. What caused the problem?

   _____

   _____

   _____

B. Review your answers to A. Complete the checklist. Then answer the questions that follow.

1. Read the list of skills. Check the boxes next to your strengths.

   ☐ creating a list of possible solutions

   ☐ researching causes

   ☐ observing possible causes

   ☐ talking to other people to gather information

   ☐ using outside sources of information to analyze causes

2. Do you want to improve any of your skills? Which ones?

   _____

3. How do you plan to improve the skills you listed in question 2?

   _____

Creating a Solution

To solve a problem, think of possible solutions and choose among them.

Sometimes finding the solution to a problem is easy. For example, imagine that you buy a new machine. The machine doesn't work when you bring it home. The solution is simple. The seller will need to fix it or replace it. Often problems are much more complex. In that case, several different solutions might be possible. This lesson presents skills that will help you choose the best possible solution.

Determine Elements for Reaching a Solution

If a problem is complex, you may have to compromise to find a solution. To **compromise** means to settle disagreements by giving up something that you need or want. You can do this by making a list of your needs and a list of your wants. The **needs** are the things that are a necessary part of the solution. The **wants** are things that might be nice to have but are not necessary as part of the solution. The solution doesn't depend on your wants. Read the following case study to learn more about needs and wants.

Case Study

Kerri meets with Pam and Chet to discuss their planned wedding reception. They say they want to invite 75 guests but can't afford such a large room. Kerri needs to find out what things the couple must have at the reception. She also wants to know what they might be willing to give up.

Discussing needs and wants is important to reaching an agreement.

Pam: Well, we have to take the smaller room. We're on a pretty tight budget. And we have to have dancing. That's a must.

Chet: And the dinner, of course.

Kerri: Does it have to be a sit-down dinner? We could do a nice buffet for you. The quality of the food would be the same. Having a buffet would be less expensive than serving the food.

Pam: We'd *rather* have the sit-down dinner, but a buffet would be all right.

Chet: What is the difference in the cost of a sit-down dinner and a buffet? And we would like to have prime rib, but we don't need to have that. Chicken or fish would be fine.

Together they have figured out the needs and wants for the reception. The smaller room and the dancing are needs. The sit-down dinner is a want. Kerri helped Pam and Chet to see that a buffet dinner would work out better. Kerri needs to create a solution based on what Pam and Chet have decided.

Sometimes it's hard to tell needs from wants. In that case, look carefully at each item.

Predict Results

You also need to look ahead and predict the results of your solution. To **predict** means to think or tell about in advance. Predicting will help you decide if your solution will, in fact, solve the problem. Make a list of **advantages,** which are the benefits, and **disadvantages,** which are the drawbacks. Make two columns. In one column, write the advantages of your solution. In a second column, write the possible disadvantages.

Listing advantages and disadvantages will also help you figure out how well your solution meets your needs and wants. Does your solution include all of your needs? Does it include all of your wants, but none of your needs? You may need to do more research to find the best solution. Think about the advantages and disadvantages of your options. Collect more information if needed. Choose the best solution you can. The best solution includes more needs than wants.

The following case study shows how Kerri weighs the advantages and disadvantages of a solution.

Case Study

Kerri is working on the solution for Pam and Chet's wedding reception. First, she needs some more information. She finds out that serving a buffet instead of a sit-down dinner will save Pam and Chet several hundred dollars. The chef tells Kerri that serving prime rib will add a lot to the total cost. Kerri is pretty sure that Pam and Chet won't think the higher cost is worth it. She finds out that the chef can offer chicken and fish at a much lower price than the prime rib. Now it's time for Kerri to weigh the information.

Following is her list of advantages and disadvantages of her solution.

Advantages

Pam and Chet will have the small room that they can afford. (The small room is a need.)

Guests will eat from a buffet. (Dinner is a need.)

They won't need many tables, which leaves room for dancing. (Dancing is a need.)

Disadvantages

They will not have a sit-down dinner. (A sit-down dinner is a want.)

They will not have prime rib. (Prime rib is a want.)

Making a list can help you think through your options.

Kerri can see that the advantages outweigh the disadvantages. The advantages include all of the couple's needs. The disadvantages include all of the couple's wants. This is the best solution because the advantages include what the couple needs. The disadvantages include only the wants, which are things that the couple is willing to give up. Kerri writes her plan for the reception based on the advantages and disadvantages. She feels she has offered Pam and Chet the very best solution to the problem.

Finding solutions isn't always easy. That's why it's important to follow the basic steps you learned about in this lesson. Start by figuring out your needs and wants. Then create possible solutions. Then weigh the advantages and disadvantages of your solutions.

Creating a Solution

23

Comprehension Check

Complete the following exercises. Refer to the lesson if necessary.

A. What is the difference between a need and a want?

_____

_____

B. What are two things you can list and compare to help you predict results of solutions?

1. _____

2. _____

C. List the two elements of reaching a solution.

1. _____

2. _____

D. Mark the following statements T (True) or F (False).

_____ 1. Finding the cause of a problem always leads to a fast solution.

_____ 2. Some solutions require information.

E. Complete each sentence. Circle the letter in front of the answer.

1. Advantages are

   a. benefits.
   b. solutions.
   c. observations.

2. In problem solving,

   a. you should use the first solution you think of.
   b. things are always more complex than you think they are.
   c. you should predict the results of your solutions.

Answer the questions following each case. Then talk about your answers with your partner or group.

Case A

Carol works at a veterinarian's office. She stocks the shelves in the waiting room. The shelves have pet food, toys, and brushes. Carol displays these items in an attractive way. The shelves are arranged to encourage customers to buy things for their pets. Carol has always arranged the shelves with the bags of food on the lower shelves. She puts the toys and brushes on the higher shelves. These items are smaller. They are at the customers' eye level. Carol's problem is that dogs smell the food on the shelves. Sometimes, they begin to chew the bags. Carol thinks of what is most important about the display. The most important thing about the display is that she needs to prevent the pet dogs in the waiting room from getting into the bags. However, she would like to design an attractive, interesting display.

What is a need for Carol? What is a want?

_____

_____

_____

Case B

Imagine that you work as a maintenance worker in a department store. The first floor of the store is being remodeled. The customers need to be able to enter the store even though there is a lot of construction near the entrance. Your supervisor has asked you to help create a solution. She says that all departments must remain open. She also says that the remodeling materials cannot be moved. She would like the plan to be inexpensive. She would like the solution to allow sales associates to work without much disruption.

1. Write a list of needs and wants for solving this problem.

_____

_____

_____

2. What are some things you would need to know to find a solution?

_____

_____

_____

3. Create a solution to the department store's problem. Write a list of the advantages and disadvantages of your plan.

_____

_____

_____

TRY IT OUT

Interview a friend or relative about a problem he or she has solved on the job. Ask questions about how the person came up with possible solutions to the problem. How did the person choose the solution? Did he or she use any of the steps you learned about in this lesson? Share the results of your interview with your class.

Think and Apply

How well do you use the skills in this lesson? Complete these exercises.

A. Think about what you learned in this lesson and answer the questions. Share your answers with your partner or your class.

1. Think about a problem that you have at work, school, or home. Make a list of your needs and wants for a solution.

    _____

    _____

    _____

2. List one solution based on your list above.

    _____

    _____

    _____

3. List advantages and disadvantages of your solution.

    _____

    _____

B. Review your answers to A. Complete the checklist. Then answer the questions that follow.

1. Read the list of skills. Check the boxes next to your strengths.
    - ☐ determining elements for reaching a solution
    - ☐ creating possible solutions
    - ☐ predicting results
    - ☐ weighing the advantages and disadvantages

2. Do you want to improve any of your skills? Which ones?

    _____

3. How do you plan to improve the skills you listed in question 2?

    _____

Lesson 4 | Making a Plan and Putting It into Action

Why does a solution require a plan?

How do you make a plan?

In order for a solution to succeed, first make a plan for putting it into action.

A **solution** is an answer to your problem or difficulty. After you find a solution, the next step is to put your solution into action with a plan. This lesson will help you create those plans.

Decide If You Need a Plan

Simple problems have simple solutions. For example, suppose you need a bulletin board to post job notices for your department. You need to request a board from the office supply department in your company. This problem is easy to solve. You need to order the board. A simple

28

problem can usually be solved quickly. Often, it can be solved by one person. It does not require a plan.

Complex problems have complex solutions. What if your work team were asked to solve a maintenance problem that affects the entire building? This kind of problem would require a complex solution. A complex problem is difficult to solve and usually involves many people. It may have more than one cause. A complex problem requires a plan to solve it.

Complex solutions usually involve many different tasks. You will need a plan if any one of the following is true:

- The problem has more than one cause.

- The solution requires many tasks.

- The solution requires the work of more than one person.

You'll need to make a plan of action for complex solutions. A **plan of action** is a method or design for a solution. The plan of action also points out who is responsible for doing each task.

Create a Plan

A plan of action is like a detailed schedule. The plan lists the amount of time allowed for each task for solving the problem. Unlike a schedule, a plan includes the job tasks for each person on the work team. Every member of the team needs to understand his or her role in carrying out the plan. Group members need to participate and stay involved in the discussion until the final plan is complete. You and your team members need to make decisions. The team also needs to **delegate,** or assign, responsibility for certain tasks to others.

Work teams need to discuss plans and divide responsibilities.

In the following case study, you'll see how one employee works with her team to form a plan of action.

29

Glen is an X-ray technician. Lately some of the machines have not been working properly. Many X rays have been taken twice because the first set didn't come out right. This costs the hospital a lot of money. Glen's supervisor has asked him to find a solution for this problem. Glen decides the equipment will be tested first thing every morning. Glen's plan of action involves all the other X-ray technicians. He meets with his team to discuss the plan. The team agrees that the morning test will be done by two people. Glen suggests that team members rotate the job so the same people won't have to check the equipment every day. Glen's next step is to create a schedule.

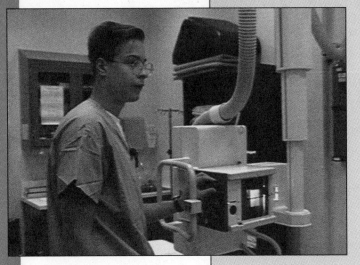

Testing and retesting equipment may solve an equipment problem.

Glen and his team came up with a solid plan of action. By delegating responsibility for testing the equipment, Glen made the plan easy to put into action.

Making the Plan Work

It's not enough just to come up with a plan. You also have to make that plan work. To do that, you may need to break down your plan into several different tasks. You may have **high-priority tasks,** which are jobs that need to be done right away. High-priority tasks are your most important tasks. If you are a nurse, responding to patients' needs is a high-priority task. **Low-priority tasks** are jobs that do not need to be done right away. Low-priority tasks are not as important as high-priority tasks. If you are planning a meeting with other nurses, ordering the food for the meeting is a low-priority task.

The following case study shows how Priscilla divides her tasks into high-priority and low-priority tasks.

Priscilla's team at REbound Shoes is working out a solution for the production problem. The machines need regular maintenance. To accomplish this solution, the team will help test and repair all the machinery on the production line. Each member of the team will be responsible for testing and repairing one area of the line. Priscilla is responsible for the area of the line where the shoes are stamped with the REbound logo. She has six trouble spots to test in her area. Three spots require cleaning. Three other spots require quick checks to make sure everything is moving properly. She knows she can't take too much time away from her regular job duties. She decides to spend the most time on the three cleaning spots. These are her high-priority tasks. The other three spots are less important. Those three spots are her low-priority tasks.

A plan involves workers in solving the problem. Following the steps in this lesson will help you to create a plan of action. These steps also show you the skills to carry out that plan.

Comprehension Check

Complete the following exercises. Refer to the lesson if necessary.

A. What is a plan of action?

_____

_____

B. List two characteristics of a complex problem.

1. _____

2. _____

C. Why might communication be an important part of a solution plan?

_____

_____

_____

D. Mark the following statements T (True) or F (False).

_____ 1. High-priority tasks are not important.

_____ 2. Listening to different points of view can often help you form solution plans.

E. Complete each sentence. Circle the letter in front of the answer.

1. If a problem is complex, it

   a. requires a complex solution and a plan of action.
   b. is not a difficult problem.
   c. does not require a plan.

2. When you delegate, you

   a. assign responsibility for a task to others.
   b. do all the tasks yourself.
   c. have solved your problem.

Answer the questions following each case. Then talk about your answers with your partner or group.

Case A

For the past eight months, the mailroom employees at Burko Publishing have been careless. The employees in other departments of the company are complaining. They say their mail is delivered late. Eileen has just been appointed the new head of the mailroom. She thinks she has a solution to the mail problem. During her first day as mailroom manager, she calls a meeting with the employees. She explains that from now on, the mail will be delivered twice a day. In addition to the regular morning delivery, there will be a second delivery in the afternoon. One of the employees asks which mailroom worker will be responsible for the afternoon delivery. Eileen tells him that it will be the same person who does the morning delivery. He tells her that the morning delivery person only works until noon each day. Eileen cuts him off sharply. She tells him that the meeting has already put the mailroom behind schedule. The next day Eileen takes a tour of the mailroom. The work space is disorganized, employees seem confused, and delivery is behind schedule.

Is the mail problem simple or complex? Why do you think Eileen's plan isn't working?

_____

_____

Case B

Josef supervises six ranch hands at the OK Cattle Ranch. Part of his job is checking the fences. He makes sure they are in good shape so that none of the cattle can get out. Last night, lightning hit a tree on the ranch and the tree smashed part of a fence. The tree will have to be removed and the fence will have to be rebuilt. Josef thinks some cows might have already escaped through the broken fence. It often takes a lot of time to round up cattle once they've escaped. He knows that the fence must be fixed today. In addition, all the regular ranch duties must be done.

How should Josef begin to create a plan? How could he decide what to do first?

_____

_____

Case C

Cara is the manager of a small deli. Each day she does most of the cleaning, ordering, and stocking. She also rings up customers at the cash register. She prepares sandwiches and soups. She makes pots of coffee and washes dishes. She's the first one there in the morning and she's the last one to leave at night. Her problem is that she feels tired and overworked. At the same time, her two employees don't have enough to do to keep them busy throughout the day. Cara often complains that her employees "don't know how to do anything." She says that if she wants something done right, she has to do it herself.

1. What is a possible solution to Cara's problem?

_____

2. How could she divide up the tasks fairly?

_____

TALK IT OUT

Work with a partner. Discuss a time when you have put a plan into action to solve a problem. You could discuss a work, school, or personal problem. Did you have high-priority tasks? Low-priority tasks? Did you delegate? Compare your plan with your partner's plan.

Think and Apply

How well do you use the skills in this lesson? Complete these exercises.

A. Think about what you learned in this lesson and answer the questions. Share your answers with your partner or your class.

1. Think about a solution to a problem you or someone you know had that required planning. Describe the plan. Was it effective? Why or why not?

   _____

   _____

2. Have you ever had to come up with a plan that involved other people? Describe any tasks that you delegated to someone else. Or describe tasks that were delegated to you.

   _____

   _____

3. Think about your goals or tasks for the week at home or at work. List some of your high-priority and low-priority tasks.

   _____

   _____

B. Review your answers to A. Complete the checklist. Then answer the questions that follow.

1. Read the list of skills. Check the boxes next to your strengths.

   ☐ creating a plan of action

   ☐ delegating

   ☐ listing high-priority tasks

   ☐ listing low-priority tasks

2. Do you want to improve any of your skills? Which ones?

   _____

3. How do you plan to improve the skills you listed in question 2?

   _____

Reviewing and Revising Plans

How do you know your solution is working?

What can you do if it isn't?

Your problem is solved only when you have made sure that your solution works.

Although you've put your solution plan into effect, your problem-solving work isn't over. You need to **monitor,** or observe, the situation to make sure the problem is being solved. If the plan isn't working, you need to revise it. To **revise** means to change. You may even have to replace the plan. This lesson will show you ways to review and revise your plans.

Check on Your Plan

It's necessary to pay attention to how things are going once your plan is in place. Often it takes time to tell whether the solution will really solve the problem.

Sometimes a solution works well at first but not so well as time goes by. Read the case study for an example.

To know if your solution is working, you need to check your plan.

Case Study

At REbound Shoes, Priscilla and her team are trying to correct the production problem. The team decided to do regular maintenance on all the machinery. They wanted to make sure the machinery was working as well as possible. Priscilla has been checking her part of the production area every day for the past week. She has six problem areas to check each day. She has allowed herself a half hour each day to do her three most important checks. She has fifteen minutes to do the other three checks. Priscilla needs to revise or change her plan because she has found she can't finish within that time. The total check takes almost an hour, so she falls behind in her regular duties. Priscilla knows she has to find another way to check the machinery and keep up with her normal job duties.

Gather Information to Change Your Plan

When you see that your plan isn't working, take action. Pay attention to details. Ask yourself *why* the plan you chose isn't working.

In the case study, Priscilla may need to check the details of her plan. Does she need to spend a half hour on the three checks? Could she spend less time? Is there a faster way to perform the work?

The answers may not be clear at first. When you are thinking about changing your plan, you may need to get more information. You may want to talk to others who are dealing with similar problems, as shown in the following case study.

Priscilla has noticed that the other members of her team are keeping up with their regular duties. They report that they have no trouble finishing their area checks each day. Priscilla wonders why she is the only one having a problem. She talks about it with another member of her team.

Jim: I think I know what's going wrong. I bet you're checking each problem area too often.

Priscilla: But I thought we wanted to be very careful.

Jim: We do, but I check each trouble spot every two days unless I find a problem. If I see a problem, I check that area again the next day. If not, I just spot-check every couple of days. It saves time.

By talking with a member of her team, Priscilla found a way to revise her plan.

Replace Your Plan

Sometimes you need to make only a simple adjustment to your plan. But what if your plan isn't working at all? Then it's important to have a backup plan. A **backup plan** is a second plan you use when your first plan doesn't work. In the following case study, Kerri needs to go to her backup plan.

Case Study

Kerri has presented her plan for Chet and Pam's wedding reception. Kerri thought that she had solved the problem of having both dinner and dancing in a small room. Her plan offered a buffet instead of a sit-down dinner. The bride and groom seemed happy with the plan, but the parents want a sit-down dinner. So Kerri's original plan won't work. She has to find a way to seat all the guests at the dinner. She must make sure the dinner is satisfying but inexpensive. Then she must find a way to use the same room for dancing. Kerri thinks carefully about the problem. She comes up with a creative solution. She meets again with Chet during his lunch hour.

Make sure you discuss a change in plans with the person involved.

Kerri: I think I've figured it out. We'll have a sit-down dinner with only one main course. Afterwards, the hotel staff will take two of the tables out of the room. That will leave just three long tables. Those can be pulled back against the wall. That way you'll have plenty of room for dancing.

Chet: What about eating the cake later? Will that be okay without those two tables?

Kerri: Well, there will still be three long tables left in the room. People who need to sit down can do so. But most people will probably stand while they eat the cake anyway. They'll be talking to you and to the other guests.

Chet: That sounds like a really good plan.

Kerri needed to revise her plan due to new information from the parents. She created a new plan that is also to the couple's liking.

Sometimes revising a plan is easy. At other times it can take more work. The important thing is to pay attention to how your plan is working. If your plan isn't working, make the necessary changes to solve the problem.

Comprehension Check

Complete the following exercises. Refer to the lesson if necessary.

A. What can you do if your plan isn't working?

_____

_____

B. Why should you monitor your solution once you've put it into action?

_____

_____

C. Mark the following statements T (True) or F (False).

_____ 1. To find out why your solution plan isn't working, you sometimes have to get more information.

_____ 2. You know in advance whether a plan will work.

D. Complete each sentence. Circle the letter in front of the answer.

1. A backup plan is

   a. a plan that doesn't work and needs to be replaced.
   b. your second choice for a solution.
   c. unnecessary in problem solving.

2. Monitoring solutions means

   a. getting rid of all your solution options.
   b. observing your plan to see if it's working.
   c. starting over.

3. To revise a solution means to

   a. monitor it.
   b. change it.
   c. put it into action.

Making Connections

Answer the questions following each case. Then talk about your answers with your partner or group.

Case A

Miguel works in the loan department of a bank. He is having trouble with one of the bank's customers. The customer is two months behind on her loan payments. The bank has sent late payment notices to the customer. Miguel tries to solve the problem. His solution is to call the customer. He makes a plan to call the customer. He is polite but firm. He tells her what might happen if she does not send her payment. He tells her she is past the payment deadline. The customer still does not pay.

1. Should Miguel continue to use this plan? Why or why not?

   _____

   _____

2. How might Miguel get more information about how to solve his problem?

   _____

   _____

Case B

Doris manages the reservations department in a hotel. There are ten reservations clerks in her department. She finds that the hotel is having trouble handling large group reservations of twenty or more people. The hotel cannot handle the large groups and the single-room reservations. The hotel cannot hold the large groups and the individuals in single rooms at the same time. One year ago, Doris had tried to solve this problem and had made a plan. She decided to keep using the same plan.

What could Doris have done in this situation?

_____

_____

Case C

Jack is an office manager at an insurance agency. One of his duties is to stock office supplies for the company. Lately he has noticed that very large amounts of supplies are disappearing. He decides to solve the problem. He calls a meeting with his staff. He tells them about the problem. He also offers a solution. He tells them not to use the company's supplies for personal use.

1. How should Jack test his solution?

   _____

   _____

   _____

2. What might Jack do if the solution doesn't work? Explain your answer.

   _____

   _____

TRY IT OUT

Interview someone about his or her job. Ask him or her to describe some problems and plans for solving them. Ask the person to explain how he or she monitors solutions to the problems. Report your findings to the class.

Think and Apply

How well do you use the skills in this lesson? Complete these exercises.

A. Think about what you learned in this lesson and answer the questions. Share your answers with your partner or your class.

1. Think of a time when you had to solve a problem at work or school. Did you use any of the problem-solving techniques mentioned in this lesson? Explain your answer.

   _____

   _____

2. Talk to a friend about a problem he or she has had. How did your friend solve the problem? What might your friend have done differently?

   _____

   _____

3. Learning how to monitor and revise solutions helps you at work and at home in your family life. Write an example of monitoring and revising solutions at home or at work.

   _____

B. Review your answers to A. Complete the checklist. Then answer the questions that follow.

1. Read the list of skills. Check the boxes next to your strengths.

   ☐ checking on my plan

   ☐ figuring out why my plan isn't working

   ☐ revising my plan

   ☐ creating backup plans

2. Do you want to improve any of your skills? Which ones?

   _____

3. How do you plan to improve the skills you listed in question 2?

   _____

Working as a Team

What kinds of problems might be better solved by a group than by one person?

What are some methods for solving problems with groups?

Some problems are better solved by a work team than by an individual.

Every problem is different. Some problems are best handled by one person. Others are more easily solved by a group. This lesson presents techniques for group problem solving.

Assess the Problem to Decide on Your Approach

To **assess** means to decide the importance or value of something. To assess a problem means to decide how complicated the problem is. Suppose you are an auto mechanic. You order supplies regularly from an auto supply company. The company provides good supplies and service except for one thing. The salesperson at the supply company does not return your phone calls. In this case, you have a problem with the salesperson. It is not a complicated problem that requires a group to solve. You can talk with the salesperson to solve the problem.

On the other hand, if your coworkers also have problems with the auto supply company, your work group may need to solve the problem together. Suppose one coworker does not like the quality of the supplies. A second coworker thinks that the supplies arrive too late. A third coworker thinks the prices are too high. In this case, you have a complicated problem with the supply company. The problem affects your whole group, so you need to solve the problem with your group.

Use Problem-Solving Methods

There are several ways to create solutions to group problems. One of the best methods is **brainstorming,** which is a way of using group participation to create ideas. This method requires every member to speak up and offer an idea. This method also takes some time to complete. Brainstorming works best when every member of the group contributes ideas, as shown in the following case study.

For a successful brainstorming session, every member must contribute ideas.

Case Study

Strongbody Athletic Gear has produced a new exercise machine. It's called the Strongbody XL. The marketing department is brainstorming the best way to market, or sell, this new product. They are discussing how to advertise the product in a national magazine.

Casey: What about a slogan like . . . "Strongbody XL, the best way to excel"? The photo could show a close-up of the machine.

Darla: That's good. Or maybe "Want to be as strong as you can be? Get the Strongbody XL."

John: What about showing a photo of a muscular man? And then the company logo and the name of the product.

Casey: That's an interesting thought.

Darla: But we want to market this product to men *and* women. I like John's idea. But I think the photo should show both men and women working out.

Brainstorming is a great way to get everyone involved in problem solving. There is another method that requires group members to participate by voting on ideas. In **private participation,** group members write their ideas and give them to a group leader or scorer. The team leader reads each idea aloud to the group. There is usually no discussion or evaluation of the ideas. Members vote on which ideas are the most effective.

An **authority** is the person who makes the final decision. The authority might be a team leader, supervisor, or boss. You might be the authority. An **authority-based decision** is a decision made by one person. Sometimes the team members get a chance to present possible solutions before the authority makes his or her final decision.

A solution may be created through a group effort or made by an authority.

Many work teams make **group-based decisions,** which means the group members work together to make the final decision. They vote for or against each idea or solution. The group must reach a **consensus,** or agreement. They discuss the options. If most of the votes are in favor of a solution, that solution will be used. The following case study is an example of a group-based decision.

Case Study

Kerri is continuing to work on her plan for Pam and Chet's wedding reception. She is trying to figure out how to include both dinner and dancing in the small room the couple has chosen. She plans to remove only two tables after the dinner. The rest of the tables will be moved back against the wall, which should leave plenty of room for dancing. Kerri doesn't want to disrupt the reception when the tables are moved. Kerri meets with the housekeeping staff and the food and beverage staff. She asks for everyone's input to solve the problem. Together they create a group-based decision or plan. Housekeeping decides to remove the two tables when the guests gather at the bride and groom's table. Later, housekeeping will move the other tables back against the wall. The food and beverage staff will clear the dishes off the tables when the guests begin to dance. At the end of the meeting, the members agree that they are happy with this solution.

Choose the problem-solving method that is best for your work team. If your group usually makes its own decisions, use the brainstorming, group-based, and private-participation methods. If your team relies on an authority to make the decisions, use the authority-based model. These problem-solving methods are used to draw ideas from group members and to make decisions. Your group will need to decide which method is best for the team.

Comprehension Check

Complete the following exercises. Refer to the lesson if necessary.

A. What does it mean to assess a problem?

_____

_____

B. What kinds of problems are best solved by groups?

_____

_____

_____

C. Complete each sentence. Circle the letter in front of the answer.

1. When one person decides on a solution for the group, he or she makes a(n)

   a. group-based decision.

   b. authority-based decision.

   c. consensus.

2. Brainstorming

   a. involves every member of the team.

   b. is done privately.

   c. is a form of authority-based decision making.

D. Mark the following statements T (True) or F (False).

_____ 1. In group-based decision making, team members must reach a consensus.

_____ 2. In private participation, group members discuss their ideas by brainstorming.

_____ 3. A group who agrees on an idea has reached a consensus.

_____ 4. Group members vote on decisions in group-based decision making.

Answer the questions following each case. Then talk about your answers with your partner or group.

Case A

Long Life Insurance has decided to hire a new food-service company to set up and run the company cafeteria. The food-service company sent a list of questions to the president of Long Life Insurance. The questions ask what kinds of food employees want. The questions also ask what times of the day the food should be served.

1. If you were the president, how would you make an authority-based decision about the food?

   _____

   _____

   _____

2. If the president gave the list of questions to employees, how would they make a group-based decision?

   _____

   _____

   _____

Case B

There is a manufacturing problem at Best Buy Motors. One of the assembly teams who puts the cars together is much slower than the others. Teams 1 and 2 can assemble a car every 28 minutes. Team 3, however, takes about 43 minutes to assemble a car.

1. Should this problem be solved by a group or by an individual worker? Why?

   _____

   _____

   _____

2. How might Teams 1 and 2 help Team 3?

_____

_____

Case C

Sharon is the program director at the public library. She is meeting with members of the special programs department. They need to plan the children's program for the summer. She invites each member to make a list of ideas for the meeting. She would like the members to vote on each idea.

1. Which two problem-solving methods would work for this group? Explain how the group would use each option.

_____

_____

_____

2. How might Sharon use this meeting to make an authority-based decision?

_____

_____

TRY IT OUT

Interview a friend or neighbor about his or her job. Ask about how problems are solved in the workplace. What problem-solving methods do they use? When are problems usually solved by one person? Take notes to record the answers. Then present your findings to the class.

Think and Apply

How well do you use the skills in this lesson? Complete these exercises.

A. Think about what you learned in this lesson and answer the questions. Share your answers with your partner or your class.

1. Describe a problem that you've had that would best be solved by a group.

   _____

   _____

2. Describe a problem that you've had that would best be handled by an individual.

   _____

   _____

3. What do you think are some advantages to brainstorming?

   _____

   _____

B. Review your answers to A. Complete the checklist. Then answer the questions that follow.

1. Read the list of skills. Check the boxes next to your strengths.

   ☐ assessing problems to decide on an approach

   ☐ choosing the best problem-solving method for your group

   ☐ brainstorming to create ideas

   ☐ using the private-participation method

   ☐ making authority-based decisions

   ☐ making group-based decisions

2. Do you want to improve any of your skills? Which ones?

   _____

3. How do you plan to improve the skills you listed in question 2?

   _____

Meeting New Challenges

How do you approach challenges?

How might problem-solving skills help you meet challenges in the workplace?

Problem-solving skills can help you meet new challenges in the workplace.

A **challenge** is an interesting task or problem that is often difficult. Every workplace presents new challenges to its workers. For example, schedules change, workloads increase, and the number of staff members decreases. Look at challenges in a positive way. How you respond to challenges can help you be successful. This lesson will show you how to deal with changes and use problem-solving skills to meet challenges.

Types of Challenges

Challenges most often involve change. The change can be large or small. You might be asked to respond in new ways to old situations. You might have to deal with totally new situations. It's important to be flexible. Be willing to try new methods to meet changes in the workplace. Is Liam flexible in the following case study?

Case Study

Liam works for the park district. He helps create newsletters and brochures about park services. He uses a computer to design them. Last week Liam's supervisor told him that the department would start using new software. The employees need to learn how to use it. Liam and his coworkers have studied the new software. They think it is very hard to understand. At first, Liam was worried about using the new software. He thought it would take too much time to learn. As Liam uses the software, he sees that it will save him time. Now Liam is excited about how the new software can help him do his job.

Learning how to use new software is an example of a challenge.

Change makes some people uncomfortable. Liam did not welcome the use of the new software at first. However, now he sees the benefit of the change and how it can help him do his job. Like Liam, look for a positive result when you approach a change.

Some of the challenges that workers face are **temporary,** which means they will last for only a short period of time. For example, you might be asked to perform a coworker's tasks for one week only. Or your project schedule might change for one day.

Other challenges are more **permanent,** which means they will last for an unlimited period of time. A new job is an example of a permanent change in your work life. A new boss is another example of a permanent change. If your department is given additional work tasks, these tasks are permanent changes. The department is expected to perform these tasks for an unlimited period of time.

View Challenges as Problems to Be Solved

The best way to handle new challenges is to face them head-on. Don't be afraid of challenges. Fear can keep you from being successful in the workplace. One good way to view a new challenge is as a problem to be solved. You might also think of a new challenge as a way of getting possible rewards on the job. Such rewards might include higher pay or career advancement. How do people view a new challenge in the following case study?

Case Study

Tomás, a supervisor, meets with Priscilla's team at the REbound Athletic Shoes factory. He thanks the team for their work on the problem of low output. The changes Priscilla and her team made have helped increase output. Tomás also tells the team that he is leaving this plant. He has taken a job at REbound's main office in New York. He introduces the team to his replacement, Lara Jackson. Lara makes a short speech about the way she wants to work with the department. She tells the team that there will be some new challenges over the next few months. REbound is going to start making a new kind of shoe. The company will also introduce a line of sports clothing. Lara tells the staff that they will need to be flexible with the changes. She hopes they will be happy about the new direction the company is taking. After the meeting, Priscilla and her coworkers discuss the situation.

Randy: It's so sudden. A new supervisor and all these new ideas.

> Priscilla: Lara seems really great. She's got a lot of energy.
>
> Lin: That's true. But I liked Tomás. I'm sorry he's leaving.
>
> Priscilla: I am too. But I'm excited about all the new possibilities.

Priscilla has the right idea. Keeping a positive attitude will help her meet the new challenges. With a negative attitude, her team would have problems working with the company changes. These challenges (or problems) are opportunities for the work team to develop and grow.

Use Problem-Solving Skills to Meet Challenges

You can use two of the problem-solving skills that you learned in Lessons 1 and 2 to meet challenges. First, identify the challenge. Second, make a plan. You can use these skills to prepare for tasks that require extra responsibility. Suppose you

Challenges are opportunities to grow and prove what you can do.

work as a teacher's aide. The teacher asks you to teach the reading class while he goes to a meeting. You are nervous about this extra responsibility. You have helped the teacher with this class before, but you have never taught the class alone. You think about it as a challenge you need to meet. First, you identify the challenge. Next, you create a plan. You might decide to use the teacher's notes or plan of instruction. Meeting new challenges in the workplace is about proving what you can do. If you have a positive attitude and use problem-solving methods, you will meet your challenges successfully.

Comprehension Check

Complete the following exercises. Refer to the lesson if necessary.

A. List two examples of temporary change in the workplace.

1. _____

2. _____

B. List three examples of permanent change in the workplace.

1. _____

2. _____

3. _____

C. Complete each sentence. Circle the letter in front of the answer.

1. A good way to view challenges is

    a. as problems to be solved.

    b. as tasks that cause you to work carefully.

    c. as changes in schedules.

2. Challenges involve

    a. dissatisfied workers.

    b. change.

    c. arguing with your supervisor.

3. Two problem-solving skills from Lessons 1 and 2 that you can use to meet new challenges are

    a. analyzing causes and finding solutions.

    b. identifying a challenge and making a plan.

    c. finding solutions and making a plan.

Answer the questions following each case. Then talk about your answers with your partner or group.

Case A

Rochester Electronics has just started a small telemarketing department. The new department will market the company's products to area businesses. The workers have already been hired. The office space for the new department will not be ready for two months. The new employees must work in a small room in the basement of the building. They are far away from other employees. Meg Peters has been named head of the telemarketing department. She wants the new employees to feel good about their jobs. She would like them to be as productive as possible.

What type of challenge is this group facing? Explain your answer.

_____

_____

Case B

Alison coaches the children's swim team at a local park. Recently she was asked to take over the entire swimming program. This job has more responsibility. Instead of one team, she will be coaching three. The duties include scheduling swim hours and hiring lifeguards. Alison will also have to oversee pool and locker room maintenance.

How might Alison view this challenge as a problem to be solved?

_____

_____

_____

Case C

Brett works for a company that rents movie and TV cameras and equipment. His job is to assemble the rental packages. For each rental, he is given a sheet that tells him what the renter needs. First, he gathers the pieces of equipment. Second, he tests them. Third, he double-checks the equipment against the rental order. Then, he packages up the equipment. Usually Brett's deadlines are very tight. One morning Brett's boss gives him the job of training Lincoln, a new employee. Lincoln knows a little about cameras, but he doesn't know anything about the company. Brett is glad his boss has faith in him. However, he's worried that today is going to be a very busy day. There are a lot of orders waiting already.

1. How might Brett approach this new challenge?

_____

_____

_____

2. If you were Brett, how would you solve this problem? Remember that you must keep up with the orders. You must also train a new employee.

_____

_____

_____

_____

TALK IT OUT

Work with a partner. Discuss some challenges or problems that you have solved at home, work, or school. Describe the challenges as temporary or permanent changes. Did you use any problem-solving skills? Did you create a plan? Share your findings with your class.

Think and Apply

How well do you use the skills in this lesson? Complete these exercises.

A. Think about what you learned in this lesson and answer the questions. Share your answers with your partner or your class.

1. Think about some of the challenges you have faced. How do you usually handle challenges? Do you try to avoid them? Do you look at them as problems to be solved? Do you view them as opportunities?

   _____

   _____

   _____

2. Imagine a challenge that you might face at work or in school. Describe how you might apply problem-solving skills to meet the challenge.

   _____

   _____

   _____

B. Review your answers to A. Complete the checklist. Then answer the questions that follow.

1. Read the list of skills. Check the boxes next to your strengths.

   ☐ being flexible in responding to challenges

   ☐ viewing challenges in a positive way

   ☐ using problem-solving skills to meet challenges

2. Do you want to improve any of your skills? Which ones?

   _____

3. How do you plan to improve the skills you listed in question 2?

   _____

Keeping Up with Technology

What is your attitude toward technology?

How do you react when you must work with new technology?

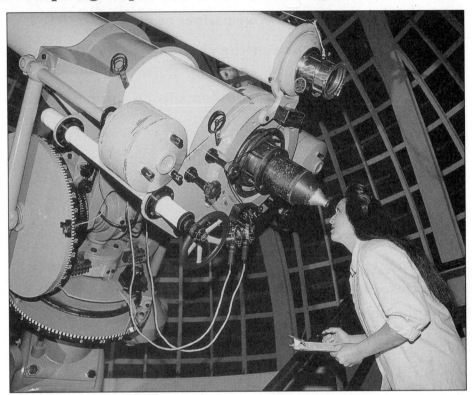

One of the challenges of today's workplace is keeping up with technology that is always changing.

Technology is the application of science for practical uses. Cars, computers, and cellular phones are forms of technology. Most employees use one or more forms of technology on the job. To be successful in the workplace, you'll need to learn and adapt to technology. This lesson will show you how to use technology to your benefit.

Ways to View Technology in the Workplace

Technology may change the way you do your job. For example, a robot may perform a task that you once did. Don't assume you'll lose your job. Being willing to learn new skills makes you a more valuable employee.

The following case study shows how Timon changes his views about technology.

Case Study

Timon just found out that the company is going to start using robots to do the manufacturing job he does now. Timon feels upset. His supervisor is explaining the situation to him.

Timon: You're telling me that a robot is going to do my job. It doesn't sound like I'm going to have a job at all.

Cariah: First of all, we're just trying out the idea. We don't know if it will work for our company. But whatever happens, please don't think you're being replaced. We're going to train you to use the robotics technology.

Timon: I guess I misunderstood. I thought that if the company had robots, it wouldn't need me. Learning how to use the robotics technology sounds great to me.

Be open to the idea of using new technology.

Timon jumped to the wrong conclusion. He assumed that the new technology meant he was out of a job. Instead it means a *change* in his job.

Some people fear technology. They are afraid that they won't be able to learn how to use it. Many companies offer on-the-job training for new equipment or systems. If you need to learn how to use a new tool, refer to a manual or book about it. A **manual** is a booklet that explains how something works. If you understand how to use the tool, it will probably make your job easier.

Remember that technology is a tool. It is meant to make your job easier and help you work more efficiently. Learning about technology isn't just a way to keep your job. It can help you advance in your career.

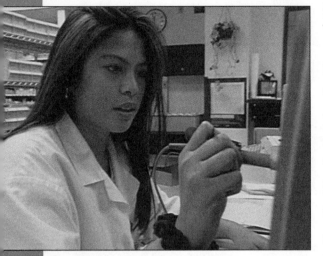

Employers value employees who know how to use technology.

Learn from Resources Inside the Company

You will learn about new technology on the job. Try to learn from more experienced workers. For example, ask a coworker to teach you to use new software. Remember to ask questions if you don't understand something. You can also refer to the print information that is part of most software packages. Use these instructions to learn the program. Also, ask a supervisor about company training for new technology. Some companies have their own "universities," which teach a variety of courses.

In the following case study, Kerri learns how to use a **spreadsheet** program to plan a wedding budget.

Case Study

Kerri is a hotel special events coordinator. She is putting the finishing touches on a plan for a wedding reception. Kerri's supervisor suggests that she use the spreadsheet program to track the costs of the reception. A spreadsheet program organizes financial information. It shows how increasing one figure affects all the other figures in a budget.

Kerri's company does not provide courses to learn the software. However, her supervisor volunteers to teach Kerri the program. Kerri decides to stay late at work to learn the program. She studies the print material at home to learn even more. Kerri knows she doesn't have to use this technology. But she figures she should learn all she can. She knows that she is learning a valuable new skill.

Learn from Resources Outside the Company

Books and magazines can help you keep up-to-date with technology. Visit a bookstore or library. Look for information about technology that your company uses. It may help for you to look for information about your specific industry, such as food service or manufacturing. Many books and magazines include sections on technology. You also might want to take courses at a technical school or adult education program. Community colleges offer courses in using software and other forms of technology. Make technology work for you and help you build your career. Employers often look for new employees who know how to use the industry's technology.

Everyone's job involves some form of technology. It may mean learning a new way of doing your job. Ask your supervisor or coworkers to help you. Sign up for company training programs and take courses. Your new skills will help you build a career.

Comprehension Check

Complete the following exercises. Refer to the lesson if necessary.

A. What is technology? Give some examples.

_____

_____

B. Complete each sentence. Circle the letter in front of the answer.

1. A good way to view new technology is

   a. as a way to help you solve problems.
   b. as a way to do less work.
   c. as a way to do more work.

2. A program that processes financial information is a

   a. computer.
   b. spreadsheet.
   c. manual.

3. A booklet that tells how something works is a

   a. spreadsheet.
   b. manual.
   c. database.

4. You can learn about technology from an inside resource such as

   a. a coworker.
   b. a community college.
   c. an adult education program.

C. Mark the following statements T (True) or F (False).

_____ 1. All companies train employees to use new technology.

_____ 2. The best way to handle new technology is to learn as much as you can.

Making Connections

Answer the questions following each case. Then talk about your answers with your partner or group.

Case A

Barrett works as an entry-level salesperson. He sells office equipment. For his first month, his sales are the highest in his department. Each month, the person who sells the most wins a prize. This month the prize is a laptop computer. Barrett doesn't think he'll use the computer for his job. He now uses a notebook to write down his sales. He uses a calendar to keep track of appointments. When he needs information about previous sales, he asks an assistant for help.

What suggestions can you make to Barrett about how to use the computer in his work?

_____

_____

_____

Case B

Matt has a job at a small garden supply company. He works in the greenhouse. His job tasks include watering the greenhouse's many plants. Matt wants to move up in his job. He's been paying attention to what other employees do. He asks a lot of questions. He's learned how to do weeding. He also knows how much fertilizer to give each plant and how to transplant. He has created a calendar on plant maintenance using the office computer. But now the company is going to buy an automatic sprinkling system. The system will do the watering that Matt used to do.

What should Matt do within the company to learn about the watering system?

_____

_____

Case C

Margaret is an interior designer. She has been home raising her children for five years. She is trying to return to work and get a job with an interior design company. She knows that most companies use computers to help them create new designs. Margaret has few computer skills.

What would you suggest to help Margaret get the job she wants?

_____

_____

Case D

Eve is a school principal. The school board is meeting to discuss technology in the schools. Board members think there should be computers in each classroom. Eve agrees that computers will help the students. But she has also spoken to the teachers. Many of them are afraid of getting new computer technology. They fear they won't be able to use it properly or to teach their students how to use it. At the end of the meeting, the school board votes to buy some computers.

What could Eve do to help teachers and students learn the new technology?

_____

_____

TRY IT OUT

Work with a partner. Visit a business and interview an employee about the use of technology on the job. Ask questions such as, "Do you use a computer in your work? Do you find a computer helpful? Does technology help you solve problems?" Prepare a written report of your interview. Share your findings with your class.

Think and Apply

How well do you use the skills in this lesson? Complete these exercises.

A. Think about what you learned in this lesson and answer the questions. Share your answers with your partner or your class.

1. How do you feel about new technology? Give some examples.

   _____

   _____

2. Imagine you have a friend who has negative feelings about new technology. What argument did you use to change your friend's mind?

   _____

   _____

3. Think of a time when you learned to use new technology. How did you get the information and skills you needed?

   _____

   _____

   _____

B. Review your answers to A. Complete the checklist. Then answer the questions that follow.

1. Read the list of skills. Check the boxes next to your strengths.

   ☐ viewing new technology in a positive way

   ☐ learning about new technology

   ☐ finding out about resources to learn technology

2. Do you want to improve any of your skills? Which ones?

   _____

3. How do you plan to improve the skills you listed in question 2?

   _____

Getting Along with Others

Do you get along well with others?

Why is getting along with others important?

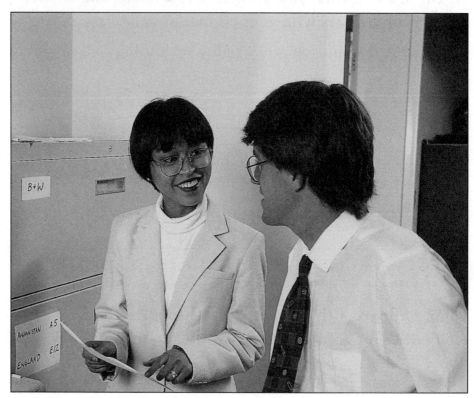

Employers want employees who know how to get along well with others.

Most of the jobs you will have in your life involve working with other people. Working with others is not always easy because we are all different. People come from different backgrounds and have different skills, work habits, and personalities. Try to understand and respect people's differences. Knowing "where people are coming from" can make your job a lot easier.

Maybe you get along well with your coworkers and customers. Even so, read the strategies that follow. You may find some new ideas to help you work with others even more smoothly.

Use Basic Strategies

An important way to get along with others is to use a polite and friendly tone. You may not always feel happy or friendly, but you shouldn't be unpleasant with others. Your coworkers are more willing to listen if you're friendly. What if you object to someone's words, behavior, or actions? Try to express yourself firmly but politely. If you do, the person may be willing to change the behavior.

When you express yourself firmly and politely, you are being assertive. **Assertive** means bold and self-confident. Asserting yourself does not mean being loud, pushy, or rude. It just means stepping forward and speaking up. You may be angry or upset with good reason, but don't lose control. If you are insulted or annoyed, speak up—politely and calmly. You have a right to ask questions and make suggestions.

Understand Cultural Differences

Today's workforce reflects a variety of cultures and points of view. Someone from a different culture may do something that you don't understand. Before you find fault with the person, look for reasons in that person's culture. Once you understand that person's point of view, you may want to change your own behavior. In the following case study, Priscilla of REbound Athletic Shoes learns how important it is to understand cultural differences.

Case Study

REbound Athletic Shoes holds a meeting after the plant has solved its production problem. At the meeting, Priscilla praises a coworker, Lon, for his help in solving the problem. Lon is Cambodian. He seems embarrassed as Priscilla tells the others what he has done. He frowns and sits very still without looking up. Priscilla is confused about Lon's behavior.

After the meeting, she tells her friend Darrell about it. Darrell explains that in the Cambodian culture, people do not like to be singled out for achievements. Accepting such praise would seem like bragging. Priscilla makes a note of this cultural difference. She decides to learn more about the cultures of her coworkers so she will not offend anyone.

When she understood more about Cambodian culture, Priscilla accepted her coworker's point of view. You should also accept different points of view. You don't have to agree with them, but respect people's opinions. Finding out why people think the way they do can help you work with them.

It may help to put yourself in the other person's shoes. Ask yourself, "What if I had to work in a place where people didn't speak my language?" Think about how you would like to be treated. Then treat others the same way. The following case study shows how.

Case Study

Aaron is a licensed practical nurse. He is caring for a very ill elderly patient. His patient's five adult children and other family members each call at least once a day to get information and give suggestions. At first, this made Aaron angry. He thought their calling kept him from doing his job properly. Then he began to think. Aaron imagined how he would feel if his own father were sick. He knew he would feel afraid and upset. He would want to make suggestions. He asked himself what kind of responses he would like to hear. Now he always answers the family's calls in a polite and caring manner. He tells them as much as he can. In short, Aaron treats the family as he would want to be treated.

Try to be patient with people who have different points of view from your own.

Get Along with Your Boss

The strategies you just learned can also help you to get along with your boss. The additional tips listed here will also help you have a good relationship with your boss.

- Be very good at your job. Complete work on time and below budget. Take extra care to do a good job.

- Learn what your boss considers important. Consider those things important, too. If your boss values good communication skills, spend some time polishing your own.

- Make sure you understand what your boss expects of you. He or she might not be completely clear. If not, make an extra effort to find out.

- Solve as many problems as you can on your own. Your boss wants you to do the job right, but doesn't want to be bothered with constant questions. A problem you solve is a problem your boss doesn't have to worry about.

- Avoid complaining about others. Take your share of the blame when something goes wrong. This shows you are honest and responsible. It will also help your boss figure out exactly what happened.

- Monitor your own performance. Be aware of feedback in response to your behavior. Feedback can be spoken, written, or communicated through body language. Act on the feedback and change your behavior if necessary. Don't wait to be told to improve.

Over time, workers who can't get along with others cost their companies time, money, and goodwill. It's no wonder that employers value most the employees who relate well to others! Perfecting your "people" skills is a wise way to use your time and energy.

Comprehension Check

Complete the following exercises. Refer to the lesson if necessary.

A. Give two basic strategies for getting along with your coworkers.

1. _____

2. _____

B. Explain what is meant by "putting yourself in someone else's shoes." Why is this important in the workplace?

_____

_____

_____

C. Answer the following questions. Circle the letter in front of the answer.

1. Which one of the following workers gets along best with others?

   a. Ralph does good work and usually gets along fine with his coworkers. But he sometimes gets upset when a team member makes a mistake. He gets red in the face, sputters, makes biting remarks, and stomps away.

   b. Aiko is generally cheerful and open-minded at work. She greets her coworkers with a smile. She seems to understand what her boss expects from her without asking.

   c. Sara regularly does impressions of coworkers during lunch. She is especially good at mimicking the behavior of her supervisors.

2. Dan, who takes phone orders for a catalog company, has made several mistakes in orders. His boss wants to talk to him about it. What should Dan do?

   a. Blame the people in the warehouse who fill the orders.

   b. Argue that the mistakes he made were just unimportant slip-ups.

   c. Accept the blame and suggest how he will improve his performance.

Making Connections

Answer the questions following each case. Then talk about your answers with your partner or group.

Case A

As a beginning telemarketer, Evelyn got in the habit of asking her boss questions. She wanted to do things right. She felt it was better to ask than to risk making a mistake. Evelyn has been on the job two years now and her work is generally praised as being good. Yet her boss delays promoting her to the next level, which has a few more responsibilities.

What could Evelyn have done to prevent the delay?

_____

_____

_____

Case B

Joellen is new at her job as a bank teller. At the end of the day, she is having trouble making her cash drawer balance. She asks Peter, a more experienced teller, for some help. He says in a sneering tone that it's her responsibility and that he has better things to do. She next asks Mazer to help her. He says, "I need to finish this paperwork first. Then I'd be happy to help you."

1. What's wrong with Peter's response?

_____

_____

2. Describe Mazer's response. Is he being helpful or not? Explain your answer.

_____

_____

Case C

Conchita's work style as a member of a data entry department is very passive. She only speaks when spoken to and seldom looks people in the eye. She does what she is told and rarely speaks up at meetings about ways to improve the department. Conchita lets her coworkers have first choice when assignments are handed out. Conchita is skilled at her work. At home she complains that she feels ignored and powerless in her job.

What could you tell Conchita to help her remedy the situation?

_____

_____

_____

_____

TALK IT OUT

Work with a group of three or four people. Think of some successful ways that you have used to get along with people at work, school, or in your neighborhood. Discuss any cultural differences and different points of view that you have known. Did you treat others the way you like to be treated? Share your experiences with your group. Then discuss them with your class.

Think and Apply

How well do you use the skills in this lesson? Complete these exercises.

A. Think about what you learned in this lesson and answer the questions. Share your answers with your partner or your class.

1. Think about bosses or teachers with whom you have had good relationships. Describe how you helped to make the relationships successful.

   _____

2. With a partner, take turns telling about times when you had trouble getting along with someone at work or at school. Brainstorm possible reasons why you didn't get along and discuss things you could have done to prevent this trouble.

   _____

3. Suppose you have a boss from another culture. What kinds of things could you do to make it easier to work for that boss?

   _____

B. Review your answers to A. Complete the checklist. Then answer the questions that follow.

1. Read the list of skills. Check the boxes next to your strengths.

   ☐ maintaining polite, friendly behavior

   ☐ understanding cultural differences

   ☐ putting yourself in other people's shoes

   ☐ being good at what you do

   ☐ learning your boss's expectations

   ☐ figuring things out by yourself and improving your own performance

2. Do you want to improve any of your skills? Which ones?

   _____

3. How do you plan to improve the skills you listed in question 2?

   _____

Lesson 10

Managing Stress

Can stress ever be good?

What are some ways you can manage stress?

You can't avoid stress, but learning how to manage it can help you on the job and in life.

Stress can affect the mind, the body, or both. **Stress** is tension caused by change. Stress can be positive. For example, imagine that you have just gotten a job that you really wanted. The new job offers more money and new challenges. But it's still change. You may feel a form of **positive stress** that allows you to work at your best. This kind of "good" stress can give you an energy boost. However, **negative stress** can keep you from doing your job well. It can also harm your health. Everyone deals with some stress as part of our everyday lives. Jobs often cause stress. You can manage or reduce your stress by using the problem-solving strategies in this lesson.

Take Care of Yourself

One of the most important things you can do to manage stress is to be good to your body. Eat right. Get enough sleep. Get plenty of exercise. Avoid drugs and alcohol. Think of your body as a complex machine. To keep it running at its best, you have to treat it well.

To be good to your body, you must also take care of your emotions. Doctors say that how we feel has a strong effect on our physical health. Save time to do things you enjoy. You might take a walk or spend time with friends. Maybe you like to play sports. Remember, *what* you do isn't as important as *how much* you enjoy yourself.

If you are suffering from negative stress, talk it over with someone you trust. Getting your feelings out in the open can help you to feel better. Another person's point of view may help you figure out the true cause of your stress.

Often stress is caused by anger or frustration. Even if you love your job, the stress can upset you. Sometimes you can use physical activity to work off negative feelings. In the following case study, Priscilla decides to work out to reduce her negative stress.

Case Study

Priscilla enjoys her job as a team leader at REbound Athletic Shoes. Lately she's been given more responsibility on the job. She's starting to feel the stress. She talks about the problem with her sister, Soledad. As Priscilla talks, she realizes she likes the challenges she faces each day. However, she thinks that the stress of her job is starting to affect her health. Soledad makes a suggestion.

Soledad: Jogging at the track every morning has helped me deal with my job stress.

Priscilla: I don't like jogging. But some of the people at REbound take aerobics classes after work. Maybe I'll sign up for a class.

Soledad: That's a great idea.

Eliminate or Control Sources of Stress

Sometimes taking care of yourself is all you need to do to feel good again. Some forms of stress call for more complex solutions. You may need to **eliminate,** or get rid of, some stress completely. If you cannot eliminate the stress, you need to control it. First, you have to analyze the cause of your stress. Is it worth the stress? Second, find a way to stop or control the situation. Ask yourself what you can do to change the situation. Read the following case study. What does Kerri do to control her stress?

Case Study

Kerri, a hotel special events coordinator, has many duties each day. Lately she has spent a lot of time planning a customer's wedding reception at the hotel. The couple's changes and requests are causing her stress. Remembering the special instructions from the other departments is also causing her stress. Kerri is worried that she is forgetting some of the details from the couple and the hotel departments. Kerri decides to stop working for a moment to think about her stress. Worrying about the details is not helping her complete her work. She decides it is not worth worrying about. To control this stress, Kerri decides to organize her work. She makes a to-do list. She uses a calendar to make sure tasks are done on time.

Organizing multiple work tasks can help you control stress.

For Kerri, the best way to control stress is to organize her work tasks. There are many other ways to manage stress. Most of the time, managing stress means making some changes in your life. It may mean that you need to take a close look at your goals. Are the demands you make on yourself reasonable? If not, you may have to **modify,** or change, your goals a bit. In the following case study, Sam modifies his goals to help him manage his stress.

Case Study

Sam has just started training to be a forklift operator. He knows that the equipment he's working with can be dangerous if misused. He worries about safety. He knows that it's important to be careful. He also realizes that his worries are causing him a lot of stress. He is afraid to make any mistakes. Sam decides that one of his goals as a beginner should be to learn as much about safety as he can. He studies the safety manual carefully. Sometimes the manual seems unclear. At those times, Sam asks his supervisor to explain it. The more he learns, the more he feels in control of what's going on. As a result, he doesn't feel so worried. Sam's supervisor is pleased that Sam has calmed down a bit. She tells Sam it's impossible to learn everything about a job in just a few days.

To control stress about safety, learn as much as you can about your work environment.

Your job is sure to include some stress. Try to make the most of positive stress. Use problem-solving strategies to reduce negative stress. Managing stress well can help to make you a valuable employee and a happier person.

Comprehension Check

Complete the following exercises. Refer to the lesson if necessary.

A. What is stress? How can it harm you?

_____

B. Name four things you can do to relieve stress.

1. _____

2. _____

3. _____

4. _____

C. Complete each sentence. Circle the letter in front of the answer.

1. Positive stress can

   a. ruin relationships with other people.
   b. give you an energy boost.
   c. take away your sense of humor.

2. Negative stress can

   a. make you feel better.
   b. harm your health.
   c. get you a better job.

3. Modifying your goals means

   a. changing your goals.
   b. getting rid of your goals.
   c. quitting your job.

D. Mark the following statements T (True) or F (False).

_____ 1. Stress is tension.

_____ 2. There's no such thing as "good stress."

_____ 3. To relieve stress, you should talk things over with someone you trust.

_____ 4. To manage stress, avoid wasting your time with activities like reading, exercising, or going to a movie.

Answer the questions following each case. Then talk about your answers with your partner or group.

Case A

Nikola is a real estate agent. He loves helping each of his clients find the right home. When he's showing property, he's relaxed and he feels great. When he's doing the paperwork, though, Nikola feels a lot of stress. It's not that Nikola doesn't know how to do the paperwork. But the process takes a lot of time. It takes Nikola away from his other duties. However, paperwork is a big part of the job.

1. Do you think Nikola can eliminate this problem?

   _____

   _____

2. What advice would you give Nikola?

   _____

   _____

Case B

Jill works as a water treatment plant operator. She is responsible for testing water quality for her community's water plant. She carries out several different water purification jobs. Recently her hours were changed. She now works an eight-hour shift starting at five o'clock in the afternoon. She gets off work at one o'clock in the morning. She usually doesn't go to sleep until about ten o'clock in the morning. She gets up again at four o'clock in the afternoon. That leaves her just one hour before work. She doesn't go to the health club anymore because she doesn't have time. Although she does the same tasks she's always done at the plant, she has been feeling a lot of stress.

1. What might be some reasons for Jill's stress?

   _____

   _____

2. What would you say to Jill to help her handle her job stress?

_____

_____

_____

Case C

Deirdre works as a clerk at Value Bank. She processes checks that customers have deposited. For a while, she has been having trouble keeping up with the work flow. Lately she has been eating lunch at her desk. She doesn't seem to have time to talk to her coworkers. When they ask Deirdre about it, she snaps at them. She says she's fine. She says she has a lot of work to do. She has started to look tired and messy at work.

1. Do you think Deirdre is suffering from too much stress? Why?

_____

_____

_____

2. What advice might you give Deirdre?

_____

_____

TRY IT OUT

Work in groups to write a booklet on stress management. First, each group member can explain a situation in which he or she has experienced and handled stress. Based on your group's experiences, put together a booklet of tips and strategies for how to manage stress. Share your booklet with the class.

Think and Apply

How well do you use the skills in this lesson? Complete these exercises.

A. Think about what you learned in this lesson and answer the questions. Share your answers with your partner or your class.

1. Think about how you handle stress. Describe the strategies that you use.

   _____

2. Describe a situation in which you or someone you know used a harmful method of handling stress. What happened? Why was the approach harmful?

   _____

3. Talk to someone you admire. Ask that person to describe a situation when he or she felt negative stress. Ask how he or she managed the stress. What problem-solving strategies did he or she use?

   _____

   _____

B. Review your answers to A. Complete the checklist. Then answer the questions that follow.

1. Read the list of skills. Check the boxes next to your strengths.
   - ☐ taking care of yourself
   - ☐ talking about stress with someone you trust
   - ☐ using physical activity to work off negative feelings
   - ☐ eliminating or controlling things that cause stress
   - ☐ modifying your goals to reduce stress

2. Do you want to improve any of your skills? Which ones?

   _____

3. How do you plan to improve the skills you listed in question 2?

   _____

Check What You've Learned will give you an idea of how well you've learned the problem-solving skills you'll need to use in the workplace.

Read each question. Circle the letter before the answer.

1. Melinda orders supplies for a ballpark. She makes sure that there are enough foods and drinks for the vendors who sell refreshments in the stands. After one week's games, she finds there is a big supply of peanuts left over. What might be a possible explanation for this?

   a. The vendors sold too many drinks.

   b. Vendors were not making enough effort to sell peanuts.

   c. Attendance at games was very high that week.

2. Barry works at a car wash. Recently the speed of the lines the cars move on has been increased. Now there is more business. But there are also more complaints from customers. The management has asked Barry to look into the problem. What should he do first?

   a. He should find out exactly what the customers' complaints have been.

   b. He should ask the workers how they like their work.

   c. He should check that the car wash's machinery is working properly.

3. Rita, Mark, Molly, and Gary are discussing the need for new equipment in their department. Rita and Mark would like to order a new fax machine. The old machine prints on poor quality paper. Molly and Gary think a new phone system should be installed. Five employees in the department share one phone and they cannot get their work done quickly. To arrive at a compromise,

   a. everyone has to think of a new plan.

   b. they should decide what are their needs and what are their wants.

   c. authority-based decisions are necessary.

4. Pat is a supervisor of a night-shift cleanup crew at a lumber mill. He creates the procedures for cleaning the mill. The crew usually can clean up each of the three parts of the mill every night. For two days, the crew has only cleaned two parts of the mill. Pat should

a. ask that the mill work fewer hours.
b. plan to clean only two parts of the mill.
c. figure out why his procedures are not working.

5. Raul is a supervisor in the mailroom of a large accounting firm. It is tax time and the firm is very busy. Raul finds that he cannot keep up with his work. Some of the employees in the mailroom are not very busy. What does Raul need to do?

a. Eliminate the things that cause stress.
b. Delegate responsibility to others.
c. Get some new technology.

6. Brainstorming can be especially effective when

a. a problem is complex.
b. everyone has had the same experiences.
c. people think that their own ideas are not helpful.

7. Lee has worked as a filmmaker for an educational company. She has enjoyed this work very much. The company needs more trained people. Lee's bosses have asked her to become the company trainer. Lee has never taught before. What should her response be?

a. She should ask the management if she can continue making films rather than teaching.
b. She should agree to teach but not put much effort into it and hope to be reassigned.
c. She should figure out how to teach her filmmaking skills and experience to others.

8. Adriana works for a clothing designer. The design company is offering classes to learn about using computers to create designs. Adriana is nervous about learning to use a computer,

but she signs up for the course anyway. She knows she will learn a new skill. Adriana is

a. afraid of computers.

b. meeting a challenge.

c. not interested in efficiency.

9. If you want to get along with others on the job, it is best

   a. not to ask them questions about themselves and their backgrounds.

   b. to learn to consider their point of view.

   c. not to do anything the boss doesn't expect you to do.

10. Blaine does copywriting for a very busy advertising firm. He often cannot sleep at night because he is thinking about his job. This is an example of

   a. suffering from negative stress.

   b. viewing challenges in a positive way.

   c. brainstorming to create ideas.

Review Chart

This chart shows you what lessons you should review. Reread each question you missed. Then look at the appropriate lesson of the book for help in understanding the correct answer.

Question Check questions you missed.	Skill The exercise, like the book, focuses on the skills below.	Lesson Review what you learned.
1. _____	Creating a list of possible solutions	2
2. _____	Gathering information	1
3. _____	Determining elements for reaching a solution	3
4. _____	Figuring out why a plan isn't working	5
5. _____	Delegating responsibility to others	4
6. _____	Brainstorming to create ideas	6
7. _____	Applying problem-solving skills to meet challenges	7
8. _____	Understanding uses of technology in the workplace	8
9. _____	Putting yourself in other people's shoes	9
10. _____	Taking care of yourself	10

Glossary

advantage: A benefit. Something that produces a favorable effect. page 22

analyze: To study a problem by carefully examining its parts. page 12

assertive: Bold and self-confident. page 69

assess: To decide the importance or value of something. page 44

authority: The person who makes the final decision. page 46

authority-based decisions: Decisions that are the result of one person. The authority might be a team leader, supervisor, or boss. page 46

backup plan: A second plan or way to accomplish a task if the first way does not work. page 38

brainstorming: A way for a group to find a solution to a problem by listing all the ideas they can think of. page 45

categories: Groups. page 5

challenge: An interesting task or problem that is often difficult. page 52

compromise: Settle a disagreement by both sides giving up something. page 20

consensus: An agreement of the majority. page 47

delegate: To assign duties and responsibilities to another person. page 29

disadvantage: A drawback or setback. Something that produces an unfavorable effect. page 22

eliminate: To get rid of. page 78

group-based decisions: Decisions that are a result of a group. Each group member votes for or against each idea or solution. page 47

high-priority tasks: Jobs that need to be completed before any other tasks. These tasks are urgent or the most important. page 30

identify: To recognize something. For example: He identified the problem. page 4

low-priority tasks: Jobs that do not need to be finished right away. page 30

manual: A booklet that explains how something works. page 61

modify: To change or make minor changes in something. page 79

monitor: To observe. page 36

needs: Things that are a necessary part of a solution. page 21

negative stress: Tension that may keep you from performing your daily tasks and may affect your health. page 76

observing: Looking closely at something. page 14

permanent: Continuing or lasting for an unlimited period of time. page 53

plan of action: A method for achieving a goal or solving a problem that includes different tasks that need to be done for the solution to work. page 29

positive stress: Tension that motivates you to work at your best. page 76

predict: To tell in advance what will happen. page 22

private participation: A type of decision-making technique that requires group members to write their ideas and give them to a group leader or scorer. The team leader reads each idea aloud to the group and members vote on which ideas will be the most effective. page 46

problem: A confusing or difficult situation or question. page 5

revise: To change. page 36

solution: An answer to a problem or difficulty. page 28

spreadsheet: A computer program that organizes data so users can see how a change in one number might affect the other numbers. page 62

stress: Tension caused by change. page 76

technology: The application of science to achieve practical solutions. Cars, computers, and cellular phones are forms of modern technology. page 60

temporary: Continuing or lasting for only a short period of time. page 53

wants: Things that you may feel the need or desire to have as part of something but are not necessary to have. page 21

Answer Key

Check What You Know (pages 1–3)

1. (b)	2. (b)	3. (c)	4. (b)
5. (a)	6. (c)	7. (c)	8. (a)
9. (c)	10. (a)		

Lesson 1

Comprehension Check (page 8)

A. Answers include that a problem is a confusing or difficult situation.

B. Answers include: gather information, organize information, interpret information.

C. Answers include: identify the problem, analyze the problem to find causes, create solutions, put the solution into action with a plan, review and revise the solution.

D. 1. (a)   2. (a)

Making Connections (pages 9–10)

Case A
1. Yes; the bakery is not producing enough pretzel packages.
2. He talks to Jeritha to gather information.

Case B
Answers include: Sarena needs to find out what is causing the arguing. She should talk to them about the conflict. She should ask questions to gather information.

Case C
1. Yes; he knows the files are disorganized.
2. Answers include: try to understand the problem; stop pretending there's not a problem; then make a plan to solve it.

Lesson 2

Comprehension Check (page 16)

A. To examine closely.

B. Answers include: think of at least five causes; then review your list and delete causes that don't seem possible.

C. Answers include: observe; talk to people; check some outside sources.

D. 1. T   2. F
E. 1. (b)   2. (a)

Making Connections (pages 17–18)

Case A
Answers include that Ellis should create a list of possible causes. He should observe Lola, and then speak with her coworkers and her.

Case B
1. Possible answers include: He could test the equipment. He could ask other technicians if they've had the same trouble. He could ask his supervisor for help.
2. Answers include: Drexel might not pay close enough attention on the job; the computer might need repair; the computer might need to be replaced; Drexel might have been hurrying through the job and made mistakes.

Case C
Answers include: Claire doesn't know where things are in the new warehouse; she may not get along with her new manager; she may not know her coworkers in the new warehouse. All of these things might be affecting her attitude.

Lesson 3

Comprehension Check (page 24)

A. Answers include: a need is something the solution depends on. A want is something that is desired but not necessary.

B. advantages and disadvantages

C. the needs and wants of the solution

D. 1. F   2. T
E. 1. (a)   2. (c)

Making Connections (pages 25–26)

Case A
Preventing the dogs from getting into the bags is a need. Designing an eye-catching, interesting display is a want.

Case B
1. Needs: Keep every department open; remodeling materials cannot be moved. Wants: Inexpensive; does not disrupt the sales associates.
2. Possible answers include: How much time the remodeling will take; how much money you can spend on solving the problem.
3. Possible solution: Design large colorful signs that let customers know about the construction. The signs tell customers that beyond the construction, the store is open for business. Possible disadvantages: Customers will see the construction area as they walk through. They may choose to go to a different store that has more eye appeal. Advantages: Customers will know that beyond the construction, the store is operating normally. Many people will still want to shop there.

Lesson 4

Comprehension Check (page 32)

A. A plan of action is a method or design for a solution.
B. Answers include that a complex problem is difficult to solve, usually requires many people, and requires a plan.
C. Possible answers include: because the solution plan may involve a team of people and they need to understand their roles.
D. 1. F   2. T
E. 1. (a)   2. (a)

Making Connections (pages 33–34)

Case A
The problem is complex. It affects the whole mailroom and employees in other departments. Possible answers include: the plan should assign tasks. The plan should include high-priority and low-priority tasks.

Case B
Possible answers include: Josef needs to meet with the other hands. They need

to set high-priority tasks and low-priority tasks.

Case C
1. Answers include: She needs to delegate more of the work to her employees.
2. Possible answers include: making a schedule for the deli employees based on the tasks mentioned; rotating duties among employees.

Lesson 5

Comprehension Check (page 40)

A. Answers include that you can make a simple adjustment or use a backup plan.
B. Answers include: to make sure that it works and keeps on working.
C. 1. T   2. F
D. 1. (b)   2. (b)   3. (b)

Making Connections (pages 41–42)

Case A
1. No. Miguel should revise his plan because it is not working.
2. Answers include: He could talk to coworkers and his manager about how they have handled similar problems in the past. He might also look at the employee handbook.

Case B
She could have monitored the situation for a while to see if her solution worked. Then she could have revised her plan when it did not work.

Case C
1. He should monitor to see if the situation improves. If the office supplies stop disappearing, he will know that he's found the solution. He will have to monitor the situation for a few months to know if the solution works over time.
2. Possible answers include: Jack will have to revise his plan. He might have employees sign for the office supplies they use. He might ask employees to offer solutions.

Lesson 6

Comprehension Check (page 48)

A. To assess a problem means to decide the importance of the problem.

B. Complicated problems that affect many people and for which solutions can be divided into many different tasks

C. 1. (b)   2. (a)

D. 1. T   2. F   3. T   4. T

Making Connections (pages 49–50)

Case A

1. Answers include: ask employees for input or make the decision by himself or herself.
2. Answers include that the group members would vote on each question and reach a consensus.

Case B

1. Answers include that the problem should be solved by a group because the problem is complicated and involves more than one person.
2. Teams 1 and 2 might provide Team 3 with ideas for improving or solutions to their problems.

Case C

1. Answers include: Private-participation and group-based methods could be used. With the private method, the group would vote on the ideas without much discussion. With the group-based method, the group would discuss the ideas before voting.
2. Answers include that Sharon could create the children's program based on the variety of options presented in the meeting.

Lesson 7

Comprehension Check (page 56)

A. Answers include: change in schedules; change in job tasks.

B. Answers include: a new job; a new boss; a new job task.

C. 1. (a)   2. (b)   3. (b)

Making Connections (pages 57–58)

Case A

Answers include: This challenge is temporary. The new work space will be finished in two months.

Case B

Possible answer: The new job will provide Alison with more responsibility. She will learn new skills. This challenge is a career opportunity.

Case C

1. Possible answers: He could approach it as a problem to be solved; he might look at it as an opportunity for possible career advancement. If he trains Lincoln well, his boss might consider him for a better position within the company.
2. Possible answer: Brett should identify the main challenge and make a plan. Brett could explain the procedures to Lincoln as he does them. He could have Lincoln help him as Lincoln learns more skills. He could use the fact that it's a busy day to his advantage.

Lesson 8

Comprehension Check (page 64)

A. Technology is the application of science for practical uses. Examples of technology include cars, phones, computers, etc.

B. 1. (a)   2. (b)   3. (b)   4. (a)

C. 1. F   2. T

Making Connections (pages 65–66)

Case A

Possible answer: Barrett can keep track of his sales. He can figure out financial information. He can use a computer calendar for scheduling sales calls.

Case B

He should ask his boss or coworkers to teach him about the system. He could ask about training programs.

Case C

Possible answers: Margaret could read books and manuals about computer programs. She could take classes to improve her computer skills.

Case D

Possible answers: Eve could make sure that the computer supply company offers training. She could schedule training sessions for the teachers who don't know how to use computers.

Lesson 9

Comprehension Check (page 72)

A. Answers include: Maintain a polite and friendly tone; assert yourself; keep your emotions under control.
B. Answers include that it means trying to feel the way someone else does and thinking about how he or she would like to be treated in a similar situation. Employees who can't get along well with others cost their companies time, money, and goodwill.
C. 1. (b)   2. (c)

Making Connections (pages 73–74)

Case A

Possible answers include: Evelyn should have worked more independently. Her frequent questions made Evelyn appear less competent than she really was.

Case B

1. Answers include that even if Peter couldn't help Joellen, he should have answered her politely. He didn't put himself in her place.
2. Answers include that Maher is helpful. He is polite and firm. He lets Joellen know that he has other work to finish. He offers to help her.

Case C

Possible answers include: Conchita's unassertive manner is hurting her on the job. Her failure to relate to her coworkers may make them suspicious of her. If she would make an effort to assert herself by expressing her opinions, she might feel less ignored.

Lesson 10

Comprehension Check (page 80)

A. Answers include: Stress is tension caused by change. It can harm relationships or physical and mental health.
B. Answers include: eat right; get plenty of sleep; exercise; avoid drugs and alcohol.
C. 1. (b)   2. (b)   3. (a)
D. 1. T   2. F   3. T   4. F

Making Connections (pages 81–82)

Case A

1. Possible answers include: No. Nikola can relieve some of the stress he feels about the paperwork, but he will probably not be able to eliminate the paperwork itself.
2. Possible answers include: Nikola should take care of himself and get plenty of exercise. Nikola might figure out a way to make the paperwork less stressful.

Case B

1. Possible answers include: She's not used to working at night. Maybe she doesn't get enough sleep. She doesn't get enough exercise because she thinks she doesn't have time.
2. Possible answers include: Jill might talk to other night workers about how they handle the hours. She also might talk to her supervisor. She could change her routine so she gets enough sleep, but still makes time to exercise regularly.

Case C

1. Yes. She doesn't take a lunch break if she is eating at her desk. She snaps at her coworkers, and she looks tired and messy.
2. Possible answers include talking things over with someone she trusts. If Diedre always has to skip lunch to get work done, she should talk to her supervisor.

Check What You've Learned (pages 84–86)

1. (b)   2. (a)   3. (b)   4. (c)
5. (b)   6. (a)   7. (c)   8. (b)
9. (b)   10. (a)